Bengal Tigers Are Awesome!

by Megan Cooley Peterson

Consultant: Jackie Gai, DVM
Wildlife Veterinarian
Vacaville, California

CAPSTONE PRESS
a capstone imprint

A+ Books are published by Capstone Press,
1710 Roe Crest Drive, North Mankato, Minnesota 56003
www.capstonepub.com

Library of Congress Cataloging-in-Publication Data
Peterson, Megan Cooley, author.
Bengal tigers are awesome! / by Megan Cooley Peterson.
pages cm. — (A+ books. Awesome Asian animals)
Summary: "Introduces readers to Bengal tigers, including physical characteristics, behavior, habitat, diet, and life cycle"— Provided by publisher.
Audience: Ages 4–8.
Audience: K to grade 3.
Includes bibliographical references and index.
ISBN 978-1-4914-3903-6 (library binding)
ISBN 978-1-4914-3922-7 (paperback)
ISBN 978-1-4914-3932-6 (eBook PDF)
1. Bengal tiger—Juvenile literature. 2. Bengal tiger—Conservation—Juvenile literature. 3. Rare mammals—Juvenile literature. [1. Tigers.] I. Title.
QL737.C23P426 2016
599.756—dc23   2014045020

Editorial Credits
Michelle Hasselius, editor; Juliette Peters, designer; Tracy Cummins, media researcher;
Morgan Walters, production specialist

Photo Credits
AP Images: Holger Hollemann/picture-alliance/dpa, 24; Capstone Press: 16; Dreamstime: Piyus Silaban, 13; FLPA: Terry Whittaker, 25; Getty Images: Andrew Parkinson, 22 Bottom, Sercan Kucuksahin/Anadolu Agency, 29 Bottom, Steve Winter, 18 Bottom; iStockphoto: andeva, 22 Top, DavidCallan, 26 Bottom, dawnn, 21 Bottom, eROMAZe, 4, 9, 21 Top, ivanmateev, 14 Top, JuliaMilberger, 28; Minden Pictures: Elliott Neep, 23, Masahiro Iijima/Nature Production, 11; Shutterstock: Anan Kaewkhammul, 20, 26 Top, 29 Top, 30 Top, 32 Top, Cover Top Left, AndreAnita, 6, dangdumrong, 10, enciktat, 19, Eric Isselee, Cover Back, Cover Left, Jackiso, 12 Bottom, Cover Right, Julian W, 27, nico99, 7 Top, RAYphotographer, 14 Bottom, Rigamondis, Design Element, RubinowaDama, 8, SasinT, 15; Thinkstock: ewastudio, 1, 5, 17, 18 Top, Jupiterimages, 12 Top, mj0007, 7 Bottom

Note to Parents, Teachers, and Librarians
This Awesome Asian Animals book uses full color photographs and a nonfiction format to introduce the concept of Bengal tigers. *Bengal Tigers Are Awesome!* is designed to be read aloud to a pre-reader or to be read independently by an early reader. Photographs help listeners and early readers understand the text and concepts discussed. The book encourages further learning by including the following sections: Table of Contents, Glossary, Read More, Internet Sites, Critical Thinking Using the Common Core, and Index. Early readers may need assistance using these features.

Printed in China.
042015   008864WMF15

Table of Contents

A Sneaky Cat

A Bengal tiger spots a deer in the rain forest. The tiger slinks through the trees and tall grass. It stays silent as it creeps up on its prey. Then the tiger leaps onto the deer.

A Bengal tiger has black, orange, and white fur. The colors help it blend in with the rising and setting sun. Those are the times tigers hunt most often. Their black stripes look like shadows in the distance. Deer, antelope, and wild pigs don't see a tiger until it's too late.

A Bengal Tiger's Body

Tigers belong to a group of animals called big cats. Lions and jaguars are also in this group. Tigers are the largest of the big cats. Adult Bengal tigers can grow to about 500 pounds (227 kilograms). They are almost 10 feet (3 meters) long. Only the Siberian tiger is bigger than the Bengal.

Bengal tigers have strong legs and shoulders. Their back legs are longer than their front legs. Bengals push off their long back legs to jump onto prey.

Their large, yellow eyes help Bengal tigers find prey easily. Tigers can see well, even at night. Their eyes have a special layer that brings in more light. The extra light helps tigers see well in the dark. At night their eyes glow when light hits this layer.

Whiskers grow on the Bengal's face
and body. They help the tiger move
around in the dark to find food.

Roar! Bengal tigers bite prey with their four canine teeth. These sharp teeth can break bone. The tiger's back teeth help it tear meat from the bone.

Bengals have four large, padded paws. The pads let them move quietly when following prey.

Long, sharp claws grow from
the Bengal tiger's paws. Tigers use
their claws to slash and hold prey.
When it's not hunting, the tiger
pulls the claws into its paws.

Life in the Forest

Wild Bengal tigers live mostly in India. They are sometimes called Indian tigers. About half of all wild tigers are Bengal tigers. Bengals make their homes in rain forests and grasslands.

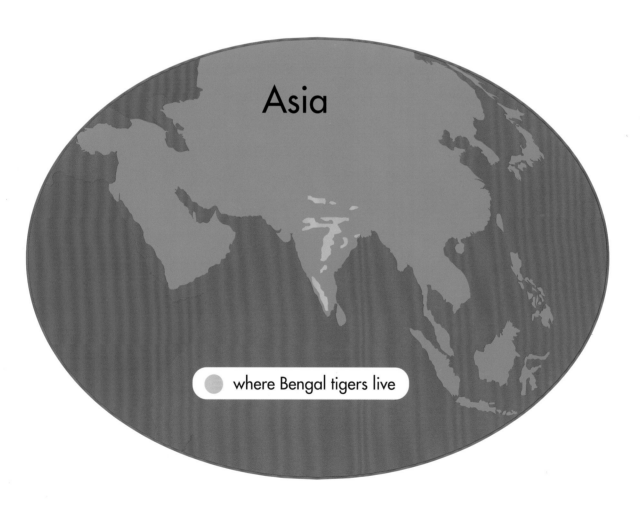

Asia

where Bengal tigers live

Bengal tigers live alone, except when mothers are raising their young. Each adult has its own home area called a range. Bengals scrape the ground and trees to mark their range. A pile of tiger poop tells other tigers to keep out.

Bengal tigers roar to keep other tigers away. Males also roar at females when it's time to mate. A Bengal tiger's roar can be heard up to 2 miles (3 kilometers) away!

Splash! Bengal tigers often live near water. They swim to cool off. They even chase prey into lakes and streams. Tigers are more at home in water than other big cats.

Bengal tigers sleep during the day. They hunt for food at night. Tigers usually hunt alone.

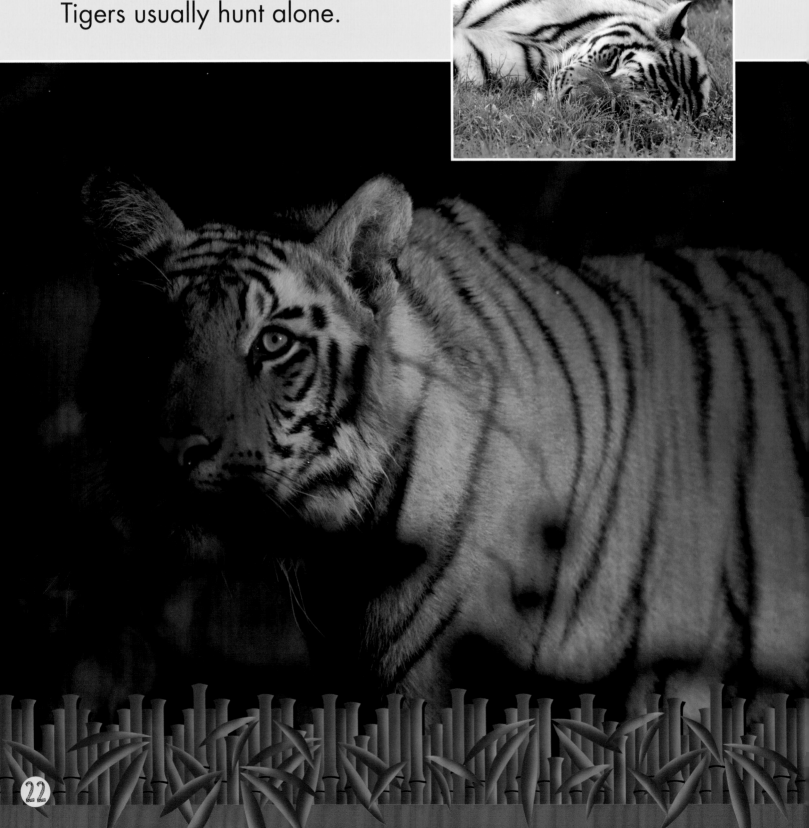

Bengal tigers eat about once or twice a week. Sometimes a Bengal can't finish a meal. It hides food in tall grass for later.

Growing Up Bengal Tiger

Female Bengal tigers give birth to a litter of cubs about three months after mating. Most litters have two or three cubs. Newborn cubs weigh about 3 pounds (1.4 kg). They can't see and have fuzzy fur.

Let's play! Bengal tiger cubs learn how to hunt by playing. They chase and jump on each other. They even pounce on their mothers. Females teach their cubs how to hunt.

Cubs stay with their mothers for about two years. In the wild, Bengal tigers can live up to 15 years.

Saving Bengal Tigers

Today all tigers are endangered. Fewer than 2,000 Bengal tigers remain in the wild. Tigers lose their homes when forests are cut down. Humans poach Bengals too.

In India land is set aside for Bengal tigers to live on. Zoos also breed Bengals. People work together to save these awesome Asian animals.

Glossary

breed (BREED)—to mate and produce young

canine (KAY-nyn)—a long, pointed tooth

cub (KUHB)—a young animal such as a tiger, cheetah, polar bear, or lion

endangered (in-DAYN-juhrd)—in danger of dying out

grassland (GRASS-land)—a large, open area where grass and low plants grow

litter (LIT-ur)—a group of animals born at the same time to the same mother

mate (MATE)—to join together to produce young

poach (POHCH)—to take animals or fish illegally

prey (PRAY)—an animal hunted by another animal for food

rain forest (RAYN FOR-ist)—a thick forest where a great deal of rain falls

range (RAYNJ)—an area where an animal mostly lives

shadow (SHAD-oh)—a dark shape made by something blocking out light

Read More

Clark, Willow. *Bengal Tigers.* The Animals of Asia. New York: PowerKids Press, 2013.

Ganeri, Anita. *Asia.* Introducing Continents. Chicago: Heinemann Library, 2014.

Marsh, Laura. *Tigers.* National Geographic Kids. Washington, D.C.: National Geographic, 2012.

Internet Sites

FactHound offers a safe, fun way to find Internet sites related to this book. All of the sites on FactHound have been researched by our staff.

Here's all you do:
Visit *www.facthound.com*
Type in this code: 9781491439036

 Check out projects, games and lots more at
www.capstonekids.com

Critical Thinking Using the Common Core

1. Bengal tigers belong to a group of animals called big cats. Name two other animals that belong to this group. (Key Ideas and Details)

2. How does the color of the Bengal tiger's fur help it hunt for prey? (Key Ideas and Details)

3. Bengal tigers are endangered. What does "endangered" mean? (Craft and Structure)

Index